ANCIENT CIVILIZATIONS

Maya

By Tami Deedrick

Steadwell Books

Raintree Steck-Vaughn Publishers

A Harcourt Company

Austin · New York

www.steck-vaughn.com

J972.81
MAYA

Published by Raintree Steck-Vaughn Publishers, an imprint of Steck-Vaughn Company.

Library of Congress Cataloging-in-Publication Data
Cataloging-in-Publication data is available upon request.

Produced by Compass Books

Photo Acknowledgments
Archive Photos, 28, 37
Corbis, cover, 10
Photo Network/Larry Dunmire, 24, 42
Root Resources/Mary Root, 12, 14, 22, 30, 38; Paul C. Hodge, 47
Unicorn Stock Photos/Abbey Sea, 34, 40
Visuals Unlimited/Bayard H. Brattstrom, title page; David Matherly, 9;
    John D. Cunningham, 17, 20; Inga Spence, 18, 26

Content Consultant
Don L. Curry
Educational Author, Editor, Consultant, and Columnist

Contents

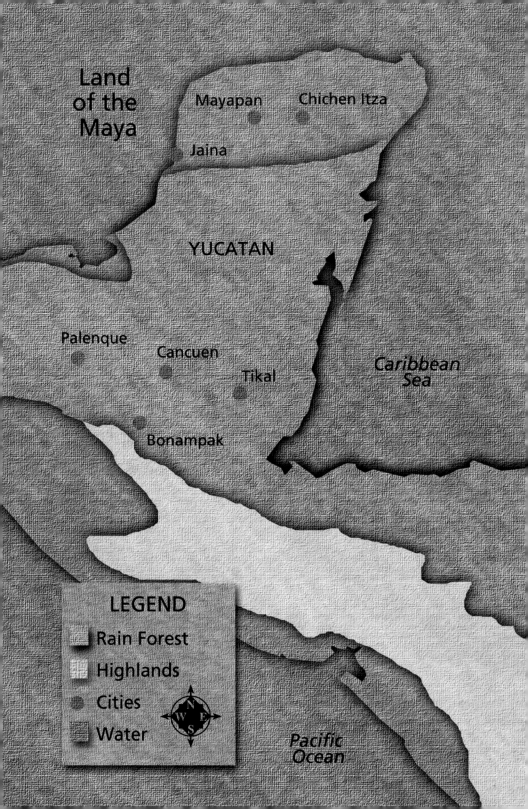

Land
of the
Maya

Mayapan   Chichen Itza

Jaina

YUCATAN

Palenque

Cancuen

Tikal

Bonampak

Caribbean
Sea

LEGEND

Rain Forest

Highlands

Cities

Water

Pacific
Ocean

Maya History

The Maya **civilization** started around 2000 B.C. A civilization is an advanced society. A society shares a common way of life. The Maya built large cities and buildings.

The Maya lived in a place called Mesoamerica. This area covers what is now southern Mexico, Guatemala, and parts of Belize and Honduras.

Archaeologists know some things about the ancient Maya from their art and writings. An archaeologist is someone who studies ancient, or old, remains. Archaeologists study the remains of Maya cities to learn what life was like for the Maya. This book is based on the information archaeologists have learned about the Maya.

THE MAYA TIMELINE

2000 B.C. to A.D. 300 **Preclassic Period**		
A.D. 300 to A.D. 900 **Classic Period**	*300*	The Maya civilization begins
	638	The great king Pacal dies
	700	Maya cities are at their peaks
	800-900	The Maya start leaving their cities
A.D. 900 to A.D. 1500 **Postclassic Period**	*980*	Toltecs invade Yucatan and make Chichen Itza their capital, The Maya are ruled by the Toltecs
	1200	Mayapan becomes the new capital
	1502	Christopher Columbus meets Maya traders
	1526	War starts between the Spanish and the Maya
	1546	Francisco de Montejo conquers the Yucatan Maya
	1697	The last Maya city is defeated
	1821	Mexico wins independence from Spain. The Maya are free.

Maya History

Ancient Maya history has three main time periods. The first is called the Preclassic Period. The Preclassic Period was from 2000 B.C. to A.D. 300. Not much is known about the people of this time. Archaeologists believe the Maya learned how to grow and water crops better during this period. They also built cities and learned to write. These things helped the Maya world spread and grow stronger.

The Classic Period lasted from about A.D. 300 to 900. Each Maya city was like its own state with its own ruling family. Each ruler passed the city on to his oldest son, who then ruled the city. There were probably 10 million Maya during this period.

The Postclassic Period lasted from about A.D. 900 until the Spanish took over the Maya area in the 1500s. During this time, Maya cities began to weaken. This might be because fighting between cities started, or there was no longer enough food or water.

Government

A ruling family was in charge of each Maya city. Priests helped them rule. The ruling family and the priests were in charge of both government and religion. Religion is belief and worship in a god or gods

Religion was at the center of much of Maya life. It helped shape their government. The priests led the people and made decisions based on religion.

The priests were powerful and educated. People believed that the priests knew the secrets of the gods. Sometimes the priests were worshiped as gods.

The priests kept the calendar and read the stars. The Maya believed that gods spoke to the priests through the way the stars moved in the sky. They thought that star movement would show when good or bad things were going to happen.

This statue shows a Maya priest giving offerings to the gods.

▲ **This painting from the Bonampak site shows the clothes of Maya warriors.**

War

War paintings at the site of Bonampak helped archaeologists learn about Maya warriors. A warrior is someone who is trained to fight. Bonampak is in the state of Chiapas, Mexico. The paintings show warriors in large headdresses. A headdress is a covering for the head. The Maya made headdresses with feathers and branches called cane.

Sometimes warriors wore cotton armor. Armor is a covering worn to keep the body safe during a fight. The Maya soaked their armor in salty water and dried it until it was stiff. Some warriors wore animal skins over their armor to make themselves look scary.

The Maya used several kinds of weapons. A weapon is a tool used for fighting. A common Maya weapon was the spear. The Maya also used clubs and a sword made from **obsidian**. Obsidian is glass found around volcanoes. The Maya used obsidian to make arrow tips, too.

The atlatl was like a wooden sword with two finger holes. The Maya put a dart on the wood. They put their fingers in the holes and raised their arms above their heads. When they pulled their arms down quickly, the darts flew through the air.

This clay statue shows how a member of the Maya royal family may have dressed.

Daily Life of the Maya

The Maya civilization had different **classes** of people. A class is a group of people who have similar jobs.

The ruling family and the nobles were the highest class. Most nobles were educated and often had a great deal of goods and property.

Priests made up the next upper class of the Maya. They were teachers and doctors. They also led the people in serving their gods.

Craftspeople were a lower class. They worked for the nobles. They built houses and temples. They sewed clothes and made jewelry.

The lowest class was the common people. They were farmers, hunters, and fishers. They provided food for all the Maya.

This statue shows how a woman from a noble family would dress.

Clothing

The Maya wore clothes made of cotton. Men wore **loincloths**. A loincloth is a long strip of cloth that wraps around the waist. The strip is pulled between the legs and tied in front. Sometimes men wore a square piece of cloth tied around the neck like a cape. It was called a pati. Rulers sometimes wore short skirts instead of loincloths. They wore sleeveless shirts with their skirts.

Women wore dresses called **huipils**. A huipil is a long piece of cloth with a hole cut for the neck. Maya women sewed the sides, leaving holes for the arms.

On special days, the Maya wore earrings and nose rings. Some wore large bands on their ankles and wrists. Colorful symbols, feathers, and decorations were woven into clothing worn on these special days.

The Maya often filed their teeth into sharp points. They filled the spaces with precious stones, such as jade. Jade is a hard, green stone.

Most Maya wore sandals. Many of the sandals were simple pieces of leather tied to the feet with rope. Nobles and priests decorated their sandals with shells or feathers. These sandals covered the heel, and thick ropes passed between the toes.

Homes

Most Maya families lived in simple houses. Homes were often made of stone or mud. Most houses were covered with a **limestone** plaster. Limestone is a hard white rock. The houses often had roofs made from palm leaves or grasses.

Houses usually had only two rooms. One room was for cooking. The other room was for sleeping. The Maya usually slept on woven mats. Sometimes cloth or an animal skin made the beds softer. The Maya covered themselves with cotton sheets.

Palaces

The Maya built palaces out of limestone that they often covered with plaster. A palace is a large, grand building belonging to a ruler. The palaces may have been used for religious ceremonies as well as a home for the ruler's family. The palaces had high ceilings and brightly painted walls. An underground room was probably used as a burial chamber.

> This is an ancient stone house built by
> the Maya.

Palenque is the most famous Maya palace. It was built to honor a great ruler named Pacal. A square tower rises from the center of the palace. It reaches 50 feet (15 m) into the air. Each ruler after Pacal made the palace larger and more beautiful to honor Pacal.

The Maya grew different kinds of corn to eat.

Food

Maya farmers grew corn as the main source of food. They also planted beans, squash, and other vegetables. Their fields were called **milpas**. The soil was rich in the rain forests and mountains. Crops grew well in the warm, rainy weather there. But the trees made farming hard. The Maya cut down the trees and set the fields on fire to burn the bushes and grass. Sometimes they built milpas by adding soil to a swamp. A swamp is an area of wet, spongy ground.

Corn could not grow without water. Finding water was easy in rain forests. But water was hard to find in the dry Yucatan. Farmers there dug deep wells or made large pots called cisterns. The cisterns caught rain. The rainwater was used later to water the crops.

Women ground corn using a **mano** and a metate. A mano is a rounded stone used like a rolling pin. A metate is a stone dish. The ground corn was used to make corn pancakes called **tortillas**. The Maya filled tortillas with beans or honey. Sometimes they mixed ground corn with water to make a drink called pozole (poh-SOH-lay).

The Maya also ate meat. They caught fish and hunted animals.

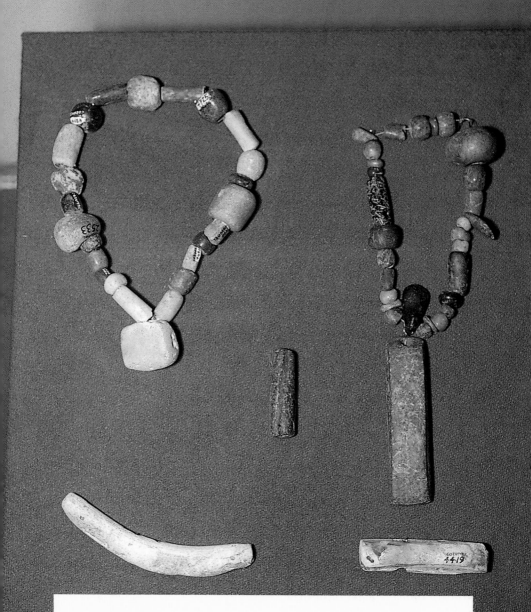

The Maya used jade and other stones to make these necklaces.

Maya Culture

The **culture** of a group of people is their ideas, customs, traditions, and way of life. The Maya expressed their culture with the things they did and made. The Maya carved stone and made **pottery**. Their clothes had colorful shapes and designs. They built great palaces. They made rubber balls for games. They wrote books that told their history.

The Maya loved to use jade. One of the most famous **artifacts** from Maya ruins is the jade mask found in Pacal's grave at Palenque. An artifact is an object made or used in the past by humans. The Maya also carved jade into statues, necklaces, and other jewelry.

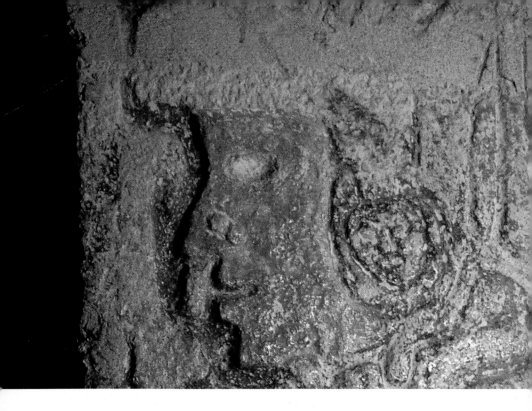

▲ **This painted carving of a warrior was on a column in a Maya temple.**

Art

The Maya used **stelae** to tell about their culture. A stela is a tall, carved post usually used as a monument. The Maya often carved one side of stelae in the image of one of their gods or their ruler. The other sides told a story with symbols. The symbols told about a person's birth, marriage, wars, death, and other important events. The Maya stelae were like history books.

The Maya were also known for their pottery. Women made bowls, plates, and cooking pots out of clay. They placed the formed clay in the fire to make it hard. Some of the pots had decorations pressed or drawn into them. Others were painted with pictures or designs. The Maya used dyes that were black, brown, orange, yellow, white, and red.

The Maya also made statues and whistles out of clay. The statues and whistles were usually in the forms of people and animals. Sometimes they were in the shape of one of the gods.

The Maya are also well known for their weaving. Most weaving was done for clothing. The Maya grew cotton and spun it into thread. They dyed the thread different colors. They wove the threads into colorful cloth full of pictures and symbols. Each town probably had its own special cloth pattern.

The remains of this Maya temple are in the Yucatan.

Architecture

Many Maya buildings looked like **pyramids** with steps on the sides and a flat top. The bottom layer was very large. Each layer was a little smaller on each side. Sometimes there were many layers. Other times there were only a few layers.

The Maya usually built a temple on top of their large pyramids. A temple was a building for worshiping the gods. The Maya added new layers if they wanted to build a new temple.

The Maya built temples with long narrow rooms, high ceilings, and high walls. The tops of the walls angled toward each other. They were topped by a single stone called a capstone. This formed a triangle-shaped structure called a corbeled arch.

Temples were always decorated with paint or carved stone. The Maya often painted or carved the same thing on all four outer walls of a temple. This way, people coming from all sides could see the same message.

This picture shows the palace next to the
Great Plaza of Tikal.

Maya Cities

Maya cities were built around large plazas.
A plaza is an open area that often has
walkways, trees, and places to sit down. The
plazas were the center of activity for the
Maya. They played games and traded goods
at the plaza. They visited with neighbors and

worshiped gods there. Temples and houses lined the sides of the plazas.

Having enough water was sometimes a problem. The Maya designed plazas so that the rain would run into special areas called aguadas (ah-GWAH-duhs). This helped the Maya gather and store water.

Tikal

Tikal is a Maya city famous for its temple pyramids. Most archaeologists think at least 10,000 people lived there. About 50,000 more probably lived around the city.

Tikal has about 3,000 buildings, including several palaces and pyramid-temples. The highest Tikal pyramid is the Temple of the Two-Headed Serpent at 213 feet (65 m) tall.

Two other temples face each other across a plaza. The temple on the east is called the Temple of the Giant Jaguar. The temple on the west is called the Temple of the Masks. Inside, archaeologists found many masks made out of wood, stone, and jade.

These statues are of gods who the Maya
believed were in charge of rain.

Religion

Religion was important to Maya life. The
Maya believed the gods would bring corn
only if they were obeyed and worshiped.

Itzamna was the most important god. His wife was Ix Chel, the goddess of weaving and medicine. All other Maya gods came from these two gods. The rain god and the corn god were two important gods because they made food grow.

The Maya told stories to explain the world around them. One story told about the creation of the world. The Two Creators called for the earth to appear and for light to shine. Trees, animals, birds, and plants appeared and started growing. But the Creators wanted people who would worship them. They made people first out of dirt, but the people could not think. Then, they made people from wood. But these people could not feel. So, they made people from corn. These people were perfect.

The Maya also believed in an afterlife. Good people who died would go to one of 13 places of rest, or heavens. Bad people who died went to one of nine places of suffering, or hells.

These ancient stone carvings tell a
Maya story.

School and Learning

Powerful Maya learned how to read and
write from the priests and nobles. Some learned
how to read the calendar and the stars.

Most of the Maya did not go to school and
never learned to read. They learned how to
farm and make cloth from their parents.

Sometimes a child showed a special talent in a craft. The parents took the child to a craftsperson and asked if the child could work with the craftsperson. If the craftsperson agreed, the child stayed there and learned.

Glyphs and Codices

Maya who could read and write used word pictures called **glyphs**. The Maya had about 500 different glyphs. With them, the Maya wrote books called **codices**. The codices told of rulers, battles, and dates in Maya history.

The Maya made paper for the codices from the bark of trees. The bark was steamed and beaten into smooth paper. The Maya used animal-hair brushes to write with dyes.

Only four books written before the 1500s survive. One of them is the Dresden Codex. It tells about the movement of the Sun and stars. It lists what the Maya thought would happen in the future. Another very important Maya book is called the Popul Vuh. It tells what the Maya believed and how they lived.

MAYA NUMBERS

0

1

5

18

20

The Maya were good with numbers. The Maya math system is based on the number 20. They may have picked 20 because that is how many fingers and toes a person has.

The Maya had three symbols for numbers. One of the symbols stood for the number zero. Most other civilizations did not have a symbol for zero. The three symbols were a shell for zero, a dot for one, and a bar for five. For example, two bars and two dots meant 12.

This illustration shows how numbers would be written with Maya symbols.

This is a Maya observatory where priests watched the stars and the Sun.

Calendar

The Maya had many calendars that all worked together. One calendar was a solar calendar. Solar means it followed the movement of the Sun. Like the modern calendar, the solar calendar had 365 days.

The Maya solar calendar had 18 months of 20 days each. The remaining five days were a month called Uayeb. The Maya believed that the days in the Uayeb were unlucky.

There was a holy calendar for planning religious ceremonies. This calendar had 260 days. Some people believed that the calendar had that many days because a woman is pregnant with a baby for 260 days. The Maya believed that each of the 260 days had a god linked to it. Some of the gods were known for being good luck, but others were known for being bad luck. So, the Maya believed that a baby born on a certain god's day would have the good luck or bad luck of that god.

Understanding how all of the calendars worked together was very hard. Only priests could read the calendars. They studied the movement of the stars and the Sun. They told people when to plant crops and what dates were lucky or unlucky.

What Happened to the Maya?

No one knows for sure what happened to make the Maya civilization start dying. But around A.D. 900 the Maya stopped carving stelae and started to leave many of their cities. The rain forests grew again and hid the cities.

In 1283, the Maya living in Yucatan moved their capital city from Chichen Itza to Mayapan. They built Mayapan with a wall around it to protect the city from enemies. About 15,000 people lived close together inside the walls.

In the early 1500s, Spanish people came to Mesoamerica to take over land and bring back riches. The Spanish found about 60 Maya cities and tried to take them over. The Spanish won some cities easily, but fought for years to win others.

The Maya who lived in the Yucatan refused to give up. They fought with the Spanish for 20 years until the Spanish capital of Merida was founded in 1546.

The Spanish talked some Maya into accepting their religious beliefs. They made

How We Know about the Maya

People today know about the ancient Maya from several sources. The Maya wrote their stories in their buildings, art, and codices. These objects and books tell many things about the Maya.

The Spanish soldiers and the missionaries who came after them shared what they knew about the Maya. A missionary is someone sent from a church to teach people about their religion.

The Maya today also have stories passed down from family to family. The stories tell what life was like for the Maya. Some modern Maya still live much like the Maya of the past.

Archaeologists have found ancient Maya ball courts where games were played.

Archaeology

Archaeologists are still finding new Maya ruins and studying them. The ruins tell about the Maya and how they lived.

Archaeologists study the writing found on buildings. At Copan, one temple has a stairway with 63 steps. Maya glyphs are carved on each step. More than 2,500 glyphs are on the stairway. Archaeologists say that the stairway contains the most Maya glyphs that they have ever found. They are still studying the glyphs today.

Maya Sites

One famous Maya site is Jaina. Jaina is an island off the coast of Yucatan. Archaeologists have found hundreds of small clay statues buried there. Most of the statues are of rulers and priests. The statues' fancy costumes are painted bright colors. Scientists believe the clay statues are of real people who lived long ago.

In 2000, scientists found another Maya ruin in a northern Guatemala jungle. The name of the city is Cancuen. It was hidden in a jungle for many years after the Maya left it. Scientists say it will take more than 10 years to discover everything in the city.

The Maya built Cancuen out of limestone. All of the buildings are still standing. The palace is huge. Archaeologists say it has three floors, 170 rooms, and 11 courtyards.

People today visit Maya ruins. They climb the pyramids to see the temples.

The Maya in the Modern World

There are at least 4 million Maya in the world today. Many of the Maya live in the same area where their ancestors lived. An ancestor is a family member who lived a long time ago. Many Maya still wear similar clothes, eat the same kinds of food, and share the same customs. One of those customs is the Dance of Resistance. This dance is performed every year. It reminds the Maya of how their ancestors fought against the Spanish 500 years ago.

The Maya have blended many of their old customs into the Roman Catholic faith. Their holidays are often held on Catholic holy days, but the Maya also add in some of their old traditions.

Today's Maya people cannot be described in only one way. Many still work in milpas and make cloth by hand. Others work in large cities and dress in business clothes. Some are wealthy, and some are poor. Some are trying to learn the newest things, while others are trying to learn and follow the old ways. The Maya's colorful history continues to be written today.

archaeologist (ar-kee-OL-uh-jist)—a scientist who studies ancient remains

artifact (ART-uh-fakt)—an object that was made or used by humans in the past

civilization (siv-i-luh-ZAY-shuhn)—an advanced society

class (KLASS)—a group of people in a society who have similar jobs

codices (KO-di-seez)—ancient books of history

culture (KUHL-chur)—the way of life, ideas, customs, and traditions of a group of people

glyphs (GLIFSS)—pictures that stand for words and objects

huipil (wee-PEEL)—a Maya dress for women

limestone (LIME-stohn)—a hard, white rock

Glossary

loincloth (LOIN-klawth)—a long strip of cloth wrapped around the waist, pulled through the legs, and tied in front

mano (MA-noh)—a rounded stone used like a rolling pin

milpa (MIL-puh)—a farm field that has been cleared from the forest

obsidian (uhb-SI-dee-uhn)—glass found around volcanoes

pottery (POT-ur-ee)—objects made of baked clay

pyramid (PIHR-uh-mid)—a triangular stone monument

stelae (STEE-lay)—tall, carved posts used as monuments

tortilla (tor-TEE-yah)—a flat, corn pancake-like bread

Internet Sites

Canadian Museum of Civilization—Maya
http://www.civilization.ca/membrs/civiliz/maya
/mminteng.html

Mexico for Kids
http://explora.presidencia.gob.mx/index_kids.
html

Minnesota State University e-Museum--Maya
http://emuseum.mankato.msus.edu/cultural/
mesoamerica/maya.html

Mysterious Places
http://www.mysteriousplaces.com/
Chichen_Itza_Page.html

**Science Museum of Minnesota's Maya
Adventure**
http://www.smm.org/sln/ma/index.html

Embassy of Mexico
1911 Pennsylvania Avenue
Washington, DC 20006

Mexican Cultural Institute
2829 16th Street NW
Washington, DC 20009

This Maya corbeled arch is more than 1,000 years old.

Index

archaeologist, 5, 7, 10, 27, 40, 41

atlatl, 11

calendar, 8, 30, 34-35

Chichen Itza, 36

Classic Period, 7

codices, 31, 39

crops, 7

glyph, 31, 40

headdress, 11

mano, 19

Mayapan, 36

Mesoamerica, 5, 36

metate, 19

milpa, 18, 19, 43

nobles, 8, 13, 30

numbers, 33

Pacal, 17, 21

palace, 16, 17, 21, 41

Palenque, 17, 21

plaza, 26

Postclassic Period, 7

pottery, 21, 23

Preclassic Period, 7

priests, 8, 13, 30, 35, 41

Spanish, 7, 36, 37, 39, 43

spear, 11

Tikal, 27

tortillas, 19

warriors, 10-11

weaving, 23